What's in a Box?

Look! Over there at the foot of the bed! Is it a chest? A trunk? A linen cabinet? A blanket box? Well, it was originally called a *coffer*, a large box with a hinged lid that was the original form of all furniture designed to hold something. In the Middle Ages, the portable trunk was the most vital piece of furniture, since moving from place to place was a way of life.

Once life settled down, larger chests evolved into ones with drawers, into cabinets, credenzas, buffets and sideboards, even beds, because nomadic ancestors slept on their trunks to protect the contents from marauders.

As civilization progressed, the practical storage unit was adapted in Germanic communities to become a dower or marriage chest. Traditionally, a father crafted the chest for a young daughter for her to fill with her handiwork, quilt tops and other household linens, in preparation for her marriage and setting up housekeeping with her husband.

Of course, the girl was destined to fill her hope chest in hopes that a special guy would come along as soon as she had it filled. In fact, a popular proverb stated, "If a girl has not made a quilt before she is 21, no man will want to marry her."

Charmingly, the process of sewing on her trousseau while her suitor billed and cooed became a form of flirtation challenged only by the coquetry of the Chinese fan. Busy little hands held in a lap complemented a young girl's perfectly erect posture as she stitched and listened to the promises of her young suitor. When she lifted her eyes from her work to peer temptingly from under fluttering eyelashes, many a troth was plighted.

Often a girl announced her engagement at a quilting bee, and a major source of entertainment for the women attending her wedding was the display of her needlework from her hope chest. Her crowning achievement, traditionally her 13th quilt, was a white bride's quilt stitched with heart designs. If a vine or floral motif was used to decorate the borders, superstition held that the design could not be broken, lest disaster follow as a self-fulfilling prophecy.

The hope chest custom seems a bit quaint today. Brides register at any number of stores and make a list of what they need or want. Grooms register at hardware and lawn care stores for their desires! What a loss of the romance of saving, sewing, hoping and courting our pursuit of "progress" has caused.

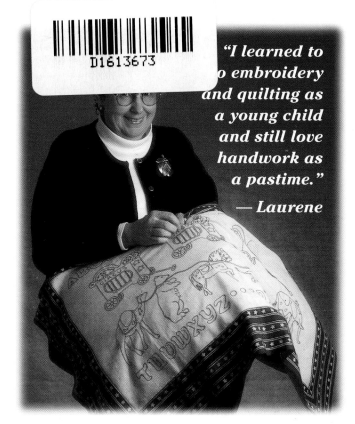

"I learned to embroidery and quilting as a young child and still love handwork as a pastime."
— Laurene

Basic How-Tos

1. Prepare blocks.
Prewash fabric to remove sizing. Mark an 'X' at the center of each square of freezer paper, on the dull side. Place the shiny side of the paper on the wrong side of the quilt block. Press with an iron to the count of '10'. The paper backing protects the pattern you are tracing, especially if you are using ink, and it stabilizes the fabric while you trace the design.

2. Trace designs.
Use the 'X' on the freezer paper as a guide to center the block over the desired pattern to be transferred. Use a .01 Red or Blue Pigma pen or a very sharp No. 2 pencil to trace the design onto the right side of the fabric. It may be easier to use a light box or to tape the pattern to a window to trace lines. Remove freezer paper after transferring the designs.

3. Embroider designs.
Use 24" lengths of floss. Separate strands, thread into a #8 embroidery needle, knot one end of floss. Use 2-ply of floss to outline stitch the large elements of the design. Use 1-ply of floss for small circles and ovals, such as eyes or berries. Trim blocks as required. Press completed blocks.

STITCHES

Outline stitch

Work from left to right. Come up at A, go down at B. Come back up at A in same hole.

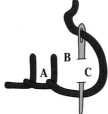

Buttonhole stitch

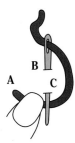

Work from left to right. Come up at A, hold thread down with your thumb and go down at B. Come back up at C with needle tip over thread. Pull stitch into place.

Chain stitch

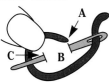

Work from right to left. Come up at A. To form a loop hold thread down with your thumb and go down at B (as close as possible to A). Come back up at C with needle tip over thread. Repeat to form a chain.

Colonial knot

Come up at A. Place needle tip under thread and wrap thread in a figure 8 around needle. Hold needle upright, pull thread firmly around needle and go down at B (as close as possible to A). Hold thread until needle is pulled through fabric.

Feather stitch

Come up at A, go down at B (to the left of A). Come back up at C with needle tip over thread to form a V. Alternate stitches from side to side.

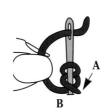

Lazy Daisy stitch

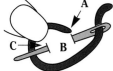

Come up at A. To form a loop go down at B (close to A). Come back up at C with needle tip over thread. Go down at D to make a small anchor stitch over top of loop.

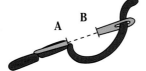

Red, White, and Blue Nin

FINISHED SIZE: 62½" wide x 74" long

SUPPLIES:
- 44" wide, 100% cotton fabrics:
  3 yards White for blocks, sashings, patches and border
  1¾ yards Blue for sashes, patches and binding
  ½ yard Red for sashing and patches
- 2 yards of White 90" wide, 100% cotton fabric for backing
- 68" x 78" piece of batting
- 3 skeins of DMC 6-ply embroidery floss to match the Red fabric
- White sewing thread
- Size 8 embroidery needle
- Red Pigma .01 pen to trace Red designs
- Sharp No. 2 pencil to trace Blue designs
- Small embroidery hoop (optional)
- Reynolds Wrap plastic coated freezer paper

CUTTING:
Cut 20 White 8" squares.
Cut 17 White 2" x 42" strips for sashing.
Cut 2 White 7" x 65" side border strips.
Cut 2 White 7" x 76" strips for top and bottom borders.
Cut 12 Blue 2" x 42" strips.
Cut Blue 1¼" wide bias binding strips.
Cut 2 Red 2" x 42" strips.
Cut 20 freezer paper 8" squares.

ASSEMBLY:
1. Follow the Basic How-Tos on page 3 to back each Whi square with freezer paper and to transfer embroidery design Embroider squares then press squares according to Bas How-Tos. Trim squares to 7½" x 7½", make certain the desig is centered on each square.

2. Use a ¼" seam allowance throughout. For patches, wit right sides facing, sew 2 sets of White and Red strips as illu trated. Press seams toward the Red strips. Sew 2 sets of Bl and White strips. Press seams toward the Blue strip.

Make 2 sets of each color combination of strips.

3. Cut each set of strips into 2" widths. Alternate colors assemble 30 Nine Patch 5" x 5" corner blocks.

Cut each set of strips into 2" wide pieces.

Sew alternating strips of color combinations together to make 30 Nine Patch blocks 5" square.

tch Quilt

. With right sides facing, sew 10 sets of White
nd Blue strips for sashing. Press seams toward
lue strips. Cut strips into 7½" widths to make
9 sashing strips.

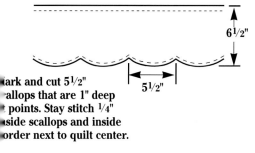

**Make 10 sets for sashings.
Cut each set of strips
into 7½" pieces.**

. With right sides facing, sew corner blocks and
ashing strips into rows as shown to make 5
ows.

. With right sides facing, alternate sashing strips
ith embroidered squares to make 4 rows. Press
eams toward the Blue strips.

. With right sides facing, sew the rows together
s shown in Assembly Diagram. Press.

. Mark 5½" scallops 1" deep along outer edges
f White border strips. Do not cut scallops until
uilting is completed, as it is easier to quilt with
traight edges.

6½"

5½"

ark and cut 5½"
allops that are 1" deep
points. Stay stitch ¼"
side scallops and inside
order next to quilt center.

. With right sides facing, sew the White 65" top
nd bottom border strips in place. Press seams toward the cen-
r of the quilt.

. Attach the White 76" side borders, mitering corners. Press
ams toward the quilt center.

. Layer backing, batting and top to form a sandwich. Baste the
yers together.

. Quilt each as desired. The quilt shown has triple chains quilt-
d along the scallop pattern of the borders.

. Trim the borders along the marked scallops.

. Bind the quilt edges with the 1¼" Blue bias strips.

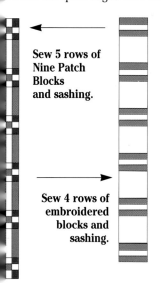

**Sew 5 rows of
Nine Patch
Blocks
and sashing.**

**Sew 4 rows of
embroidered
blocks and
sashing.**

*The blocks in this
beautiful quilt contain
a special meaning.
From ages 3 to 6
Martha embroidered
all the squares. The
quilt was put together
by her grandmother.*

RED, WHITE AND BLUE NINE PATCH QUILT ASSEMBLY DIAGRAM

Red Patches Quilt

FINISHED SIZE: 70½" wide x 78" long

SUPPLIES:
- 44" wide, 100% cotton fabrics:
  - 2⅓ yards White for blocks
  - 2¾ yards Red for blocks and borders
  - 4⅔ yards White for backing and binding
- 75" x 82" piece of batting
- 10 skeins DMC 6-ply embroidery floss to match Red fabric
- White sewing thread
- Size 8 embroidery needle
- Red Pigma .01 pen or sharp No. 2 pencil
- Small embroidery hoop (optional)
- Reynolds Wrap plastic coated freezer paper

CUTTING:
Cut 45 White 9" squares.
Cut 4 White 1½" x 80½" binding strips.
Cut 2 White 17½" x 84" pieces for backing.
Cut 1 White 42" x 84" piece for backing.
Cut 2 Red 2" x 68" top and bottom border strips.
Cut 2 Red 2" x 78½" side border strips.
Cut 45 Red 8" squares.
Cut 45 freezer paper 9" squares.

A classic jewel

of the Redwork

quilt tradition,

this quilt has

a variety of

block designs,

ranging from

birds and animals

to geometric flowers

and people.

ASSEMBLY:

1. Follow the Basic How-Tos on page 3 t back each White square with freeze paper and to transfer embroidery design Embroider and press squares according t Basic How-Tos. Trim squares to 8" x 8 make certain the design is centered o each square.

Sew squares together to form rows.

2. Use a ¼" seam allowance throughou With right sides facing, sew alternatin Red and White squares into rows as illu trated. Press seams toward the Re blocks.

3. Sew the rows together as shown i Assembly Diagram. Press seams open.

4. With right sides facing, sew the Red 68 top and bottom border strips in plac Press seams toward borders.

5. Attach the Red side borders in th same manner. Press seams toward bo ders.

6. To assemble backing, sew a Whit 17½" backing piece to each side of th 42" piece, right sides facing. Press seam toward the center piece.

7. Layer backing, batting and top to for a sandwich. Baste the layers together.

8. Machine quilt diagonal lines across th quilt 1¼" apart. Repeat to quilt diagon lines across the quilt in the opposi direction to form a crosshatch pattern.

9. Trim the backing and batting to th edge of quilt top.

10. Bind the quilt edges with the 1½ White strips.

RED PATCHES QUILT ASSEMBLY DIAGRAM

Red + Blue Patches

FINISHED SIZE: 65" wide x 84" long

SUPPLIES:

- 44" wide, 100% cotton fabrics:
  - ¾ yards Red for blocks
  - ¾ yards Blue for blocks
  - 4 yards White for blocks and borders
  - 5 yards White for backing and binding
- 70" x 89" piece of batting
- 3 skeins of DMC 6-ply embroidery floss to match the Red fabric
- 3 skeins of DMC 6-ply embroidery floss to match the Blue fabric
- White sewing thread
- Size 8 embroidery needle
- Red Pigma .01 pen to trace Red designs
- Sharp No. 2 pencil to trace Blue designs
- Small embroidery hoop (optional)
- Reynolds Wrap plastic coated freezer paper

CUTTING:

Cut 12 Red 8" squares.
Cut 12 Blue 8" squares.
Cut 24 White 9" squares
Cut 2 White 1¼" x 68" binding strips.
Cut 2 White 1¼" x 86" binding strips.
Cut 2 White 15" x 90" pieces for backing.
Cut 1 White 42" x 90" piece for backing.
Cut 2 White 12½" x 45½" strips for the top and bottom borders.
Cut 2 White 10½" x 84½" side border strips.
Cut 24 freezer paper 9" squares.

ASSEMBLY:

Follow the Basic How-Tos on page 3 to back each White square with freezer paper and to transfer embroidery designs. Embroider 12 squares with Red floss and 12 squares with Blue floss then press squares according to Basic How-Tos. Trim squares to 8" x 8", make certain the design is centered on each square.

Use a ¼" seam allowance throughout. With right sides facing, sew embroidered squares into rows as shown in Assembly Diagram. Press seams toward the solid Red and Blue squares.

With right sides facing, sew the rows together as shown in Assembly Diagram. Press.

With right sides facing, sew the White 45½" top and bottom border strips in place. Press seams toward the center of the quilt.

Attach the White 84½" side borders in the same manner. Press seams toward the quilt center.

To assemble backing, sew a White 15" backing piece to each side of the 42" piece, right sides facing. Press seams toward the center piece.

Layer backing, batting and top to form a sandwich. Baste the layers together.

Quilt each as desired. The quilt shown has fans quilted in each corner and the same quilting pattern is used for each border.

Trim the backing and batting to the edge of quilt top.

10. Bind the quilt edges with the 1¼" White strips.

An appealing combination of Red, White and Blue creates a patriotic style quilt. Fill each square with your choice of designs.

RED AND BLUE PATCHES QUILT ASSEMBLY DIAGRAM

Cut 36 White 9¾" x 9¾" squares.

Cut 2 White 1½" x 79" binding strips for the top and bottom.

Cut 2 White 1½" x 87" binding strips for the sides.

Cut 2 White 2" x 66½" strips for th inner top and bottom borders.

Cut 2 White 2" x 74¾" strips for th inner side borders.

Cut 2 White 2" x 73½" strips for th outer top and bottom borders.

Cut 2 White 2" x 85¾" strips for th outside borders.

Cut 18 White 2¼" x 42" strips for the pieced middle borders.

Cut 15 White 1⁷⁄₁₆" x 42" strips for the 9-patch blocks.

Cut 144 White 3¼" squares for the 9-patch blocks.

Cut 2 White 20" x 90" pieces for backing.

Cut 1 White 42" x 90" piece for backing.

Cut 15 Red 1⁷⁄₁₆" x 42" strips for th 9-patch blocks.

Cut 9 Red 2" x 42" strips for the pieced middle borders.

Cut 36 freezer paper 9¾" squares.

Redwork Irish Chain Quilt

Combine blocks with five Nine Patch blocks and four White blocks to make a traditional Irish Chain quilt. Add the pieced border of squares set on point to frame it!

FINISHED SIZE: 77" wide x 85¼" long

SUPPLIES:

- 44" wide, 100% cotton fabrics:
  2½ yards Red for blocks and borders
  7¼ yards White for blocks and borders
  5¼ yards White for backing and binding
- 81" x 90" piece of batting
- 8 skeins DMC 6-ply embroidery floss to match the Red fabric
- White sewing thread
- Size 8 embroidery needle
- Red Pigma .01 pen or sharp No. 2 pencil
- Small embroidery hoop (optional)
- Reynolds Wrap plastic coated freezer paper

REDWORK AND NINE PATCH QUILT ASSEMBLY DIAGRAM

1. Follow the Basic How-Tos on page 3 to back each White square with freezer paper and to transfer embroidery designs. Embroider then press squares according to Basic How-Tos. Trim squares to 8¾" x 8¾", make certain the design is centered on each square.

2. Use a ¼" seam allowance throughout. With right sides facing, sew 1⁷⁄₁₆" strips for the 9-patch blocks into sets as illustrated below. Make 5 sets of each combination of strips. Press the seams toward the Red strips.

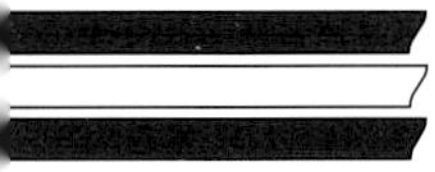

Make 5 sets of each combination of colors

3. Cut the assembled 9-patch strips into 1⁷⁄₁₆" widths as shown below.

Cut each set of strips into 1⁷⁄₁₆" pieces

4. With right sides facing, alternate the pieces of color sets to assemble Nine Patch blocks. Make 180 blocks 3¼" square. Press each block.

Make 180 Nine Patch blocks 3¼" square

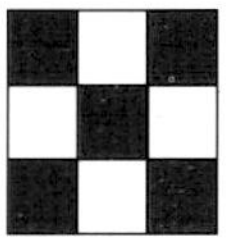

5. Alternate 9-patch blocks with 3¼" White squares to make 36 blocks 8¾" square. Press squares.

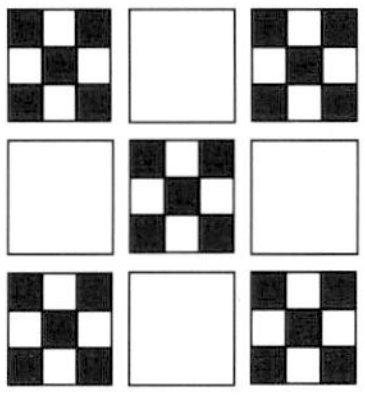

Make 36 blocks 8¾" square

6. With right sides facing, sew the rows together as shown in Assembly Diagram. Press well.

7. Sew pieced border strips together as shown to make 9 sets. Press seams toward Red strips. Cut 2" wide strips across each set.

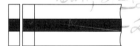

Cut each set of strips into 2" wide strips

8. Align seams to stagger strips as illustrated. Sew strips together. Press the seams in one direction.

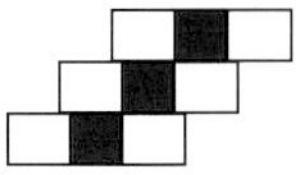

Stagger strips, aligning seams of Red patches. Sew strips together.

9. Trim the edges at each side of the assembled strips. Leave a ¼" seam allowance at each side of each Red square as shown.

Trim away White squares. Leave a ¼" seam allowance.

10. With right sides facing, sew the White 66½" top and bottom border strips in place. Press seams toward the borders of the quilt.

11. Attach the White 74¾" side borders in the same manner. Press seams toward the borders.

12. Add the pieced borders across the top and bottom of the quilt. Press. Attach the pieced side borders.

13. Sew the 73½" top and bottom outer borders in the same manner, then attach the outer side borders.

14. To assemble backing, sew a White 20" backing piece to each side of the 42" piece, right sides facing. Press seams toward the center piece.

15. Layer backing, batting and top to form a sandwich. Baste the layers together.

16. Quilt as desired.

17. Trim the backing and batting to the edge of quilt top.

18. Bind the quilt edges with the 1½" White strips.

A Little History of Embroidery...

In 802, the Bishop of Worchester granted a lease for life on a 200 acre farm to embroideress **Eanswitha** of Hereford, England, providing she wash, maintain and replace the garments of priests in the cathedral church.

In 16th Century England, noblewoman **Bess of Hardwick** shared a passion for embroidery with **Mary Queen of Scots** - literally. Married to one of Mary's jailers, Bess and Mary worked together on several pieces, which they both signed. Many of these pieces hang at Oxburgh Hall in Norfolk. Mary even had her own embroiderer, **Pierre Oudry** (a man!), who followed her to Scotland during her captivity.

William Broderick (another man!) was the official embroiderer to James I of England. In 1611 he stitched roses and crowns on 268 red coats for the royal servants and the next year he rendered the bride's chamber draperies and linens for the King's daughter, Princess Elizabeth.

In the late 1700s two English women developed embroidery techniques which resembled brushstrokes. In 1771, **Mary Knowles** rendered a portrait of George III and a self portrait of herself working on his portrait. The Queen still owns both these works. **Mary Linwood** refused 3,000 guineas for her portrait of Salvador Mundi; she bequeathed the picture to Queen Victoria. Her portrait of Napoleon I hangs in London's Victoria and Albert Museum.

America's own **Betsy Ross** (an upholsterer by trade!) suggested a simpler 5-point star to replace the original 6-point one for the flag she embroidered. The national emblem was adopted on July 14, 1777.

Jessie Rowan Newbery pioneered the modern approach to embroidery in the Glasgow School in the 1890s. She insisted on clean designs with emphasis on lettering and spacing. She designed comfortable clothes for herself in direct contrast to the tight corsets that were the fashion of her day. (God bless her!)

Louisa Frances Pesel of Bradford, Yorkshire, went to Greece to become the head of the Royal Hellenic Schools of Needlework and Lace in Athens in 1903. She returned to England in 1907 to inspire and lead the Winchester Broderers, who worked cushions and kneelers for Winchester Cathedral from 1931 to 1936, the forerunner of such projects.

In 1906 the 'Society of Certificated Embroideresses' was formed by past members of the Royal School of Needlework in England. The name was changed to **Embroiderer's Guild** in 1920. The American chapter was founded in 1958 and has been a separate entity since 1970.

CUTTING:

Cut 16 White 9" x 9" squares.
Cut 24 White 4½" x 11¾"
    sashing strips.
Cut 2 White 4½" x 57½" strips for
    inner top and bottom borders.
Cut 2 White 4½" x 65½" strips for
    inner side borders.
Cut 9 Blue 4½" x 4½" squares for
    the small corner blocks.
Cut 32 Blue 6½" x 6½" squares for
    triangles.
Cut 2 Blue 11" x 65½" strips for the
    outer top and bottom borders.
Cut 2 Blue 11" x 85½" strips for the
    outer side borders.
Cut remaining Blue fabric into 1½"
    bias binding strips.
Cut 16 freezer paper 9" squares.

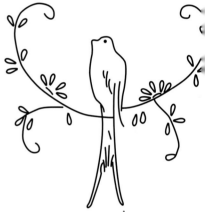

Blue Diamond Quilt

*'Redwork' stitched in 'Blue' is a wonderful
combination for beautiful quilts. Any design can
be translated to this pleasing color. Combine
embroidered squares, triangles and strips
to create an elegant display of your talents.*

FINISHED SIZE: 85" wide x 85" long

SUPPLIES:
- 44" wide, 100% cotton fabrics:
    2⅔ yards White for blocks and sashings
    4 yards Blue for small blocks, triangles, binding and borders
- 90" wide, 100% cotton fabric:
- 2½ yards White for backing
- 90" x 90" piece of batting
- 5 skeins DMC 6-ply embroidery floss to match the Blue fabric
- White sewing thread
- Size 8 embroidery needle
- Blue Pigma .01 pen or sharp No. 2 pencil
- Small embroidery hoop (optional)
- Reynolds Wrap plastic coated freezer paper
- 10" and 7" dinner plates for scallops (see step 8)

BLUE DIAMOND QUILT ASSEMBLY DIAGRAM

ASSEMBLY:

1. Follow the Basic How-Tos on page 3 to back each White square with freezer paper and to transfer embroidery designs. Embroider then press squares according to Basic How-Tos. Note that the design on the quilt shown was embroidered square with the block, creating an off-kilter look. You may wish to place your designs on the point within the square.

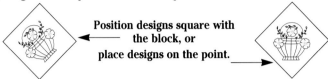

Position designs square with the block, or place designs on the point.

Trim squares to $8\frac{1}{2}$" x $8\frac{1}{2}$", make certain the design is centered on each square.

2. Cut the $6\frac{1}{2}$" Blue squares in half diagonally to create 64 right triangles. Use a $\frac{1}{4}$" seam allowance throughout. With right sides facing, sew 4 triangles to each embroidered block as illustrated.

Cut each $6\frac{1}{2}$" square in half to make 64 triangles.

Sew a triangle to each corner of each embroidered block.

3. With right sides facing, sew White sashing pieces to $4\frac{1}{2}$" Blue squares to make 3 sashing strips as shown. Press the seams toward the Blue squares.

Make 3 sashing strips

4. Sew White sashing pieces between design blocks to make 4 rows. Press the seams toward the Blue triangles.

Make 4 rows of blocks

5. With right sides facing, sew the rows together as shown in Assembly Diagram. Press.

6. Attach the White top and bottom border strips. Press seams toward the center of the quilt. Attach the White side borders in the same manner. Press.

7. Sew the Blue top and bottom outer borders in the same manner, then attach the outer side borders. Press seams toward the borders.

8. Mark a 10" circle on the outer borders at each corner of the quilt. Mark 7" scallops between the corners across the top, bottom and down each side. Do not cut the scallops until after the quilting is done.

Mark and cut 7" scallops that are 1" deep at points.
Stay stitch $\frac{1}{4}$" inside scallops and inside border next to quilt center.

$10\frac{1}{2}$"

7"

9. Layer backing, batting and top to form a sandwich. Baste the layers together.

10. Quilt as desired.

11. Trim the outer edges along the marked scallops.

12. Bind the quilt edges with the Blue bias strips.

Reindeer Wall Quilt

Rudolph's nose isn't the only part of him that's Red! Stitch this charming deer design on fabric, then surround the center with red plaid borders for festive Holiday or cabin decor.

Photo of Reindeer wall quilt is on page 15

FINISHED SIZE: 24" x 21"

SUPPLIES:

- 44" wide, 100% cotton fabrics:
  - $\frac{1}{2}$ yard White with Red stripe for center block
  - $\frac{3}{4}$ yard Red plaid for borders, backing and binding
- 26" x 23" piece of batting
- 1 skein of DMC 6-ply embroidery floss to match the Red border fabric
- Red sewing thread
- Size 8 embroidery needle
- Red Pigma .01 pen or sharp No. 2 pencil
- Small embroidery hoop (optional)
- $18\frac{1}{2}$" x $15\frac{1}{2}$" piece of plastic coated freezer paper

CUTTING:

Cut a White $18\frac{1}{2}$" x $15\frac{1}{2}$" piece for the center.
Cut 2 Plaid 4" x $17\frac{1}{2}$" strips for the side borders.
Cut 2 Plaid 4" x $24\frac{1}{2}$" strips for top and bottom borders.
Cut a Plaid 26" x 23" piece for backing.
Cut remaining Plaid fabric into $1\frac{1}{4}$" strips for binding.

ASSEMBLY:

1. Follow the Basic How-Tos on page 3 to back center fabric with freezer paper. Trace the pattern on pages 22 and 23 onto the center of the fabric.

2. Use 1 ply of floss and outline stitch to embroider design. Trim fabric to $17\frac{1}{2}$" x $14\frac{1}{2}$". Press well.

3. Use a $\frac{1}{4}$" seam allowance throughout. With right sides facing, sew the top and bottom border strips in place. Press the seams toward the border strips.

4. With right sides facing, attach side borders. Press.

5. Layer backing, batting and top to form a sandwich. Baste the layers together. Quilt around all motifs.

6. Trim the backing and batting to the edge of quilt top.

7. Bind the quilt edges with the $1\frac{1}{4}$" strips.

Helpful Hint

Do not carry the floss across large areas on the back of the design, Tie off and start again. The Red and Blue threads carried across the back of an unstitched White square will show through on the front.

Sheets and Pillowcases

Crisp red and white sheets with matching pillowcases and a flowing leaf design are sure to guarantee sweet dreams. What a perfect gift idea for newlyweds ... or for you and your mate on your own anniversary!

SUPPLIES:
- Purchased sheets and pillowcases with Red borders
- 3 skeins of DMC 6-ply Red embroidery floss to match the Red borders
- Size 8 embroidery needle
- Red Pigma .01 pen or sharp No. 2 pencil
- Embroidery hoop (optional)

INSTRUCTIONS:
1. Locate and mark the center of the top sheet just below the border. Align the dashed line at one end of the embroidery pattern on page 20 at marked center, transfer design. Repeat to transfer design across one half of sheet. Place the dashed line at the other end of the pattern at marked center. Transfer design across other half of sheet. Transfer design across one end of each pillowcase in the same manner.
2. Use one ply of floss to embroider designs. Press each piece well.

> ### Helpful Hint
> When working outline stitches, hold the thread toward you until you come to an upward curve. Begin holding the thread away from you to create a smoother and prettier curve with your stitches.

Clothes Hanger Cover

Pretty, practical and protective! The perfect idea for preserving a precious garment, this hanger cover will delight the clotheshorse in your life.

FINISHED SIZE: 5" x 19"

SUPPLIES:
- 44" wide, 100% cotton fabrics:
  ¼ yard muslin for front and back
  ¼ yard Red for binding
- 1 skein of DMC 6-ply Red embroidery floss to match the Red fabric
- White sewing thread
- Size 8 embroidery needle
- Red Pigma .01 pen or sharp No. 2 pencil
- Small embroidery hoop (optional)
- 9" x 18" piece of Reynolds Wrap plastic coated freezer paper

CUTTING:
Cut 2 muslin 9" x 22" pieces for front and back on fold.
Cut Red 1" wide bias strips for binding.

> ### Helpful Hint
> To transfer a lazy daisy stitch for a flower petal, do not trace the whole petal. Just put a dot at each end of it for placement. The floss will not cover the line drawn if you trace the whole petal.

ASSEMBLY:

1. Follow the Basic How-Tos on page 3 to back one muslin piece with freezer paper and to transfer embroidery design. Make certain design is centered on fabric. Embroider design with 1 ply of floss. Press.

2. Center embroidered muslin piece over pattern for hanger cover. Trace solid outline for front as indicated on pattern. Make certain the design is centered on the piece. Press well.

3. Center plain muslin piece over pattern for hanger cover. Cut along the dashed inner curve for the back indentation as shown on pattern. Sew bias binding along the curved line of the back indentation.

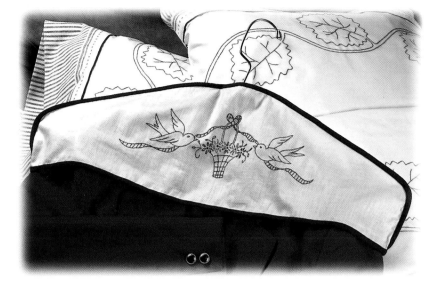

BACK
Right Side

4. With wrong sides facing, stitch bias binding around top and sides of cover. Begin at the bottom on one side and sew to the bottom on the other side.

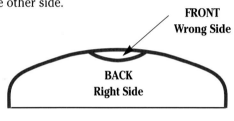

FRONT
Wrong Side

BACK
Right Side

5. Sew binding around the lower edges.

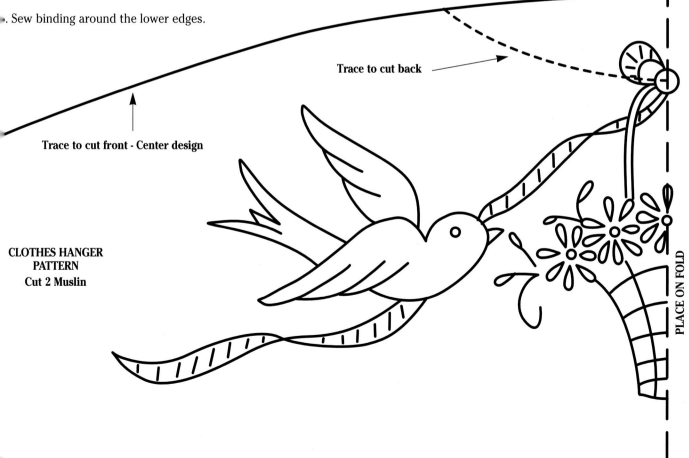

Trace to cut back

Trace to cut front - Center design

CLOTHES HANGER PATTERN
Cut 2 Muslin

PLACE ON FOLD

Heart Sachet

Sweet memories are easy to recall when you share this miniature scented sachet pillow with a friend.

FINISHED SIZE: 3" x 3"

ADDITIONAL SUPPLIES:
- Pattern on page 88
- Scented oil or potpourri

ASSEMBLY:
Follow Basic Instructions, except fill halfway with fiberfill. Add scented oil or potpourri to center, stuff firmly. Stitch opening closed. For garland, string each heart on a 24" long piece of 6-ply floss. Tie floss ends together in a bow between each heart.

Heart Scissors Holder

Every crafter has a favorite "cut-up" as a friend. Reward the laughter they bring to your life with a small gift.

ADDITIONAL SUPPLIES:
- Pattern on page 88
- Two 6" x 6" Red fabric squares
- Two 6" x 6" squares of thin batting
- One more 6" x 6" square of plastic coated freezer paper

ASSEMBLY:
1. Back one Red square with freezer paper and transfer outline of holder onto it.
2. With right sides facing, layer muslin squares then a batting square to form a sandwich. Sew layers together along outline and trim seam. Turn to right side. Press and stitch opening closed. Repeat with Red squares and other batting square.
3. Lay the padded front and back pieces together with embroidered design facing. Use 2 ply of floss to buttonhole stitch through all layers around sides and bottom to attach front to back. Work buttonhole stitches across the top of each of the front and back pieces.

Heart Projects

BASIC SUPPLIES (for each heart):
- Two 6" x 6" muslin squares
- 1 skein of DMC 6-ply Red embroidery floss
- White sewing thread
- Size 8 embroidery needle
- Red Pigma .01 pen or sharp No. 2 pencil
- Polyester fiberfill
- Small embroidery hoop (optional)
- One 6" x 6" square of plastic coated freezer paper

BASIC INSTRUCTIONS (for each project):
1. Follow the Basic How-Tos on page 3 to back muslin squares with freezer paper. Trace the outline of the heart and transfer embroidery design onto squares. Embroider designs with 1 ply of floss, then press squares according to Basic How-Tos.
2. Use a ¼" seam allowance throughout. With right sides facing, layer muslin squares. Sew layers together along outline of heart pattern, leaving an opening at one side as shown on pattern. Trim seam to ⅛".
3. Turn heart to right side. Press and stuff firmly with fiberfill. Stitch opening closed.
4. Use 2 ply of floss to buttonhole stitch around all sides.

Heart Pin

Wear your heart on your shoulder as the perfect fashion accessory any time of year. And it's a great Valentine's gift!

ADDITIONAL SUPPLIES:
- Small pin back

ASSEMBLY:
Follow Basic Instructions for each pin. Sew pin back in place.

Leave open

Heart Pin Cushion

Cupid used an arrow to pierce hearts ... Your favorite seamstress will enjoy this pretty and practical accessory!

ADDITIONAL SUPPLIES:
- Pattern on page 88
- One 9" x 9" muslin square
- Two 9" x 9" square of plastic coated freezer paper
- Purchased heart shaped or round pincushion stand.

ASSEMBLY:
1. Follow Basic Instructions to transfer design and outline of Heart Sachet to muslin square. Embroider design and outline with 1 ply of floss. Press square.
2. Follow instructions provided with the pincushion stand to complete the project.

Child's Pinafore

Cute is for little girls. Embroider these simple designs on a readymade dress or pinafore!

SUPPLIES:
- Purchased White pinafore with scalloped hem
- 1 skein of DMC 6-ply Red embroidery floss
- Size 8 embroidery needle
- Red Pigma .01 pen or sharp No. 2 pencil
- Small embroidery hoop (optional)

INSTRUCTIONS:

1. Follow the Basic How-Tos on page 3 to transfer embroidery designs onto the dress. Center bodice pattern and lengthen or shorten the distance between the flowers as needed to fill the space. Trace a single flower onto each scallop around the hem. Hint: It may be easier to use a light box to trace the designs.

2. Embroider designs with 1 ply of floss. Press.

PINAFORE BODICE PATTERN
Lengthen or shorten spaces between flowers to fill bodice as desired.

PINAFORE HEM PATTERN

Bird Pillow

These love birds will be right at home in your home!

FINISHED SIZE: 20" x 20"   Instructions for Reindeer wall quilt are on page 11

SUPPLIES:
- 44" wide, 100% cotton fabrics:
  - ½ yard Off White for center block
  - ⅔ yard Floral for borders and backing
- 20" x 20" pillow form
- 1 skein of DMC 6-ply embroidery floss to match the Red in the fabric
- Red sewing thread
- Size 8 embroidery needle
- Red Pigma .01 pen or sharp No. 2 pencil
- Small embroidery hoop (optional)
- 15½" x 15½" piece of plastic coated freezer paper

CUTTING:

Cut a White 15½" x 15½" piece for the center.
Cut 2 Floral 3½" x 14½" strips for the side borders.
Cut 2 Floral 3½" x 20½" strips for top and bottom borders.
Cut a Floral 20½" x 20½" piece for backing.

ASSEMBLY:

1. Follow the Basic How-Tos on page 3 to back center fabric with freezer paper. Trace the pattern on pages 24 and 25 onto the center of the fabric.

2. Use 1 ply of floss and outline stitch to embroider design. Trim fabric to 14½" x 14½". Press well.

3. Use a ¼" seam allowance throughout. With right sides facing, sew the top and bottom border strips in place. Press the seams toward the border strips.

4. With right sides facing, attach side borders in the same manner. Press the seams toward the border strips.

5. With right sides facing, sew backing and top together to form a pocket. Leave a 16" opening along one side.

6. Turn to right side. Press. Insert pillow form. Sew opening closed by hand.

Sew pillow front to backing with right sides facing. Use ¼" seam allowance. Leave a 16" opening on one side.

Leave open

Miniature Floral Quilt

This quilt is a great take-along project.
The designs are traced onto one piece
of fabric and embroidered. As a last step
the squares are cut apart for assembly.

FINISHED SIZE: 16" x 20"

SUPPLIES:
- ⅔ yard 44" wide, 100% cotton muslin
- 2 skeins DMC 6-ply Red embroidery floss
- White sewing thread
- Size 8 embroidery needle
- Red Pigma .01 pen or sharp No. 2 pencil
- Small embroidery hoop (optional)
- Reynolds Wrap plastic coated freezer paper
- Straight edge or ruler

CUTTING:
Do not cut muslin until instructed.
Cut a piece of freezer paper 24" x 42".

INSTRUCTIONS:
1. Follow the Basic How-Tos on page 3 to back muslin with freezer paper.

2. Mark a grid of twenty 5" x 5" squares across fabric. Center each square over a flower design to transfer embroidery patterns. Make certain one design is centered in each of the marked blocks. Remove the freezer paper.

3. Embroider designs with 1 ply of floss according to Basic How-Tos. Cut apart the 5" squares. Press squares.

4. Use ½" seam allowance to sew squares together, right sides facing. Press seams to one side. Trim seams to ¼".

5. Fold back ¼" around all outer edges, press. Fold back ¼" again around outer edges and stitch hem in place.

6. Feather stitch along inner seams and around outer edges as shown in photo.

Center your choice of flower designs in each square of the miniature quilt.

Circus Wall Quilt

Cotton candy! Clowns! Popcorn!
Elephants, lions and camels! The midway!
Bring the glee of the circus parade to a wall
near you - or your favorite ferris wheel friend.

FINISHED SIZE: 27" x 39"

SUPPLIES:
- 44" wide, 100% cotton fabrics:
  ⅔ yard Osnaberg or Lin'n Spun for center block
- Red and Blue Striped fabric for borders
  ⅔ yard if crosswise stripe, or
  1¼ yards if lengthwise stripe
- 1 yard fabric to coordinate with center for backing
- 28" x 42" piece of batting
- 2 skeins of DMC 6-ply embroidery floss to match the Red stripe of border fabric
- Red sewing thread
- Size 8 embroidery needle
- Red Pigma .01 pen or sharp No. 2 pencil
- Small embroidery hoop (optional)

Satin Stitch

Come up at A, go down at B. Come back up at C to make a straight stitch. Repeat to fill the outlined shape.

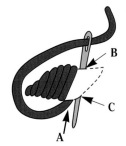

Helpful Hint

To make sharp, clean corners, come up at A, go down at B. Come up at C (at corner) with needle tip over thread. Go down at D to secure loop at corner, come back up at B.

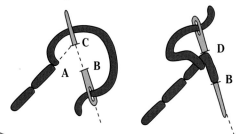

CUTTING:

Cut 2 Striped 4½" x 39½" strips for top and bottom borders.
Cut 2 Striped 4½" x 27½" strips for side borders.
Cut 4 Striped 1½" wide strips for binding.

ASSEMBLY:

Follow the Basic How-Tos on page 3 to transfer the embroidery designs on pages 21 onto the center of the 22" x 44" center block fabric.
Use 2 ply of floss and outline stitch to embroider designs. For small eyes and small circles, use 1 ply of floss. Satin stitch filled areas with 1 ply of floss. Trim fabric to 19½" x 31½", making certain the design is centered on the block. Press well.
Use a ¼" seam allowance throughout. With right sides facing, sew the top and bottom border strips in place. Press the seams toward the border strips.
With right sides facing, sew side borders in the same manner. Press seams toward border strips. Miter corners.
Layer backing, batting and top to form a sandwich. Baste the layers together.
Quilt around all motifs, letters and numbers.
Trim the backing and batting to the edge of quilt top.
Bind the quilt edges with the 1½" strips.

OVERLAY PATTERNS FROM PAGES 20 - 25 FOR THE CIRCUS

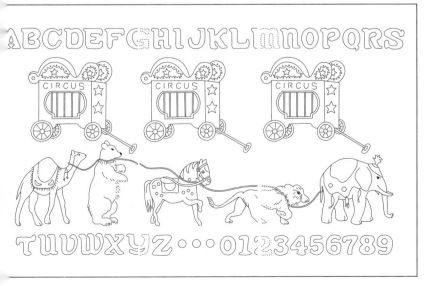

Traditional bird and heart motifs are found on old hope chests. These were symbols for "Love, Marriage and Happiness" in Pennsylvania Dutch communities. A particular plumed bird - the distelfink - was painted or carved onto some early American hope chests to insure good luck in the home of the newlyweds. Oak leaf patterns on hope chests were insurance of strength, health and a long life. Stylized flower and heart shapes on a hope chest wished the new householders love and romance. A pattern of an 8-pointed star and tulips predicted fertility, good will and abundance within a house.

CIRCUS

OVERLAP DASHED LINES WITH
PATTERN ON PAGES 22 AND 23

CIRCUS

OVERLAP DASHED LINES WITH
PATTERN ON PAGES 24 AND 25

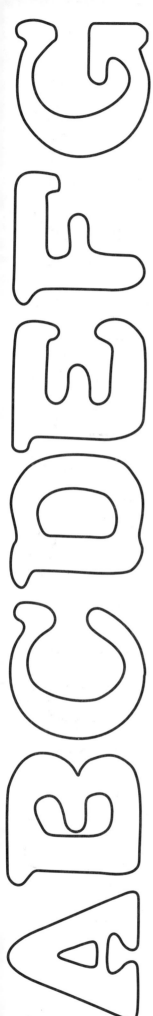

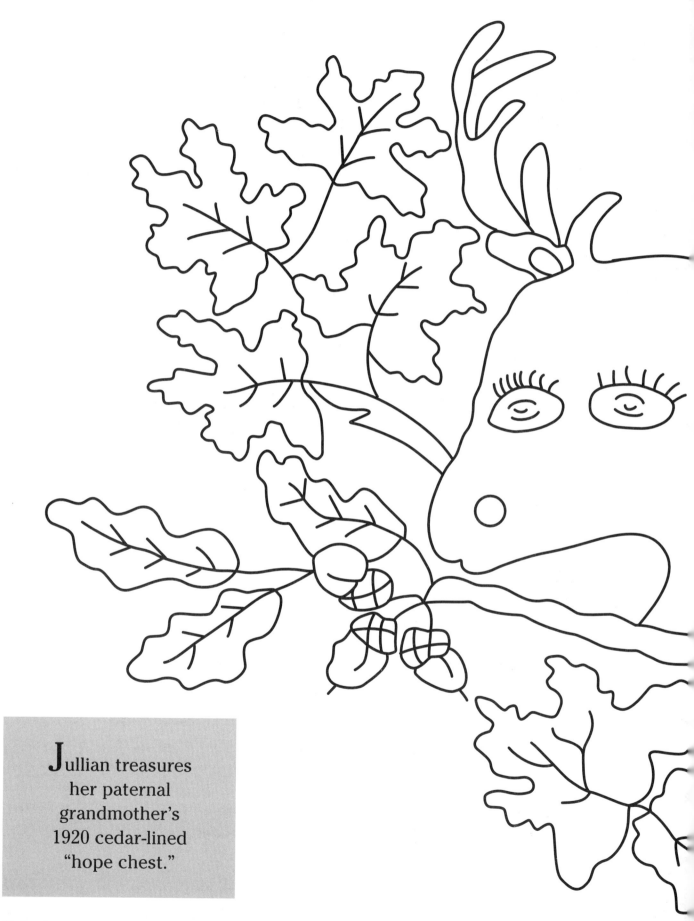

J ullian treasures
her paternal
grandmother's
1920 cedar-lined
"hope chest."

**BIRDS PILLOW
INSTRUCTIONS ON PAGE 15**

My mother said, "A bird in the hand
Is worth two in the bush."
I asked "What does that mean?"
She just said, "Hush!"

I was given a sock monkey made from
my father's work sock. He had a red
mouth and a funny little bell on his tail.
Some days he swung from a bell.

**SHEETS AND PILLOWCASES
INSTRUCTIONS ON PAGE 12**

In times long past,
Waving each cloth covered arn
Windmills ground grain
And gave Holland unique charn

Photo on page 8

HOME
SWEET
HOME

Photo on page 10

Photo on page 10

Photo on page 7

Lighthouse standing in plain sight
Newly painted red and white,
Shine your beacon bright
And keep sailors safe at night.

Roses are red,
Violets are blue.
Blooming on your bed,
They tell of love that's true.

Photo on page 7

Photo on page 6

Photo on page 5

Photo on page 8

Photo on page 6

Remember that the hope chest was just that: By the time a young woman filled a trunk with her needlework, she "hoped" that her future husband would appear. Traditionally, this was by the time she turned 16.

Photo on page 8

Photo on page 7

Photo on page 8

Photo on page 10

Photo on page 10

*Daisy, daisy, can you
Tell me if my love is true?*

Photo on page 5

Photo on page 10

...terflies spend summer hours
...ping nectar from the flowers.

Photo on page 6

Photo on page 8

Spider, Spider spinning free,
Spin a web to catch dreams for me.

Photo on page 8

INDIAN CONGRESS and VILLAGE

A loyal dog
Is child's best friend.
Love him and feed him,
He's true to the end.

Photo on page 5

Red sails upon the sea,
Bring my love home safely to me.

Photo on page 6
and page 10

Photo on page 8

a branch in spring,
A love bird pair
in harmony sing
their joy to share.

Photo on page 10

Photo on page 8

Pat received her
grandmother's
cedar-lined
hope chest as
a wedding gift.

Photo on page 10

Blue bird sitting in a tree,
: a song of happiness for me.

Blue Bird

'hoto on page 10

Photo on page 6

Photo on page 6

01234
56789

1934

A basket filled with flowers red
Blooms in glory on my bed.

Photo on page 6

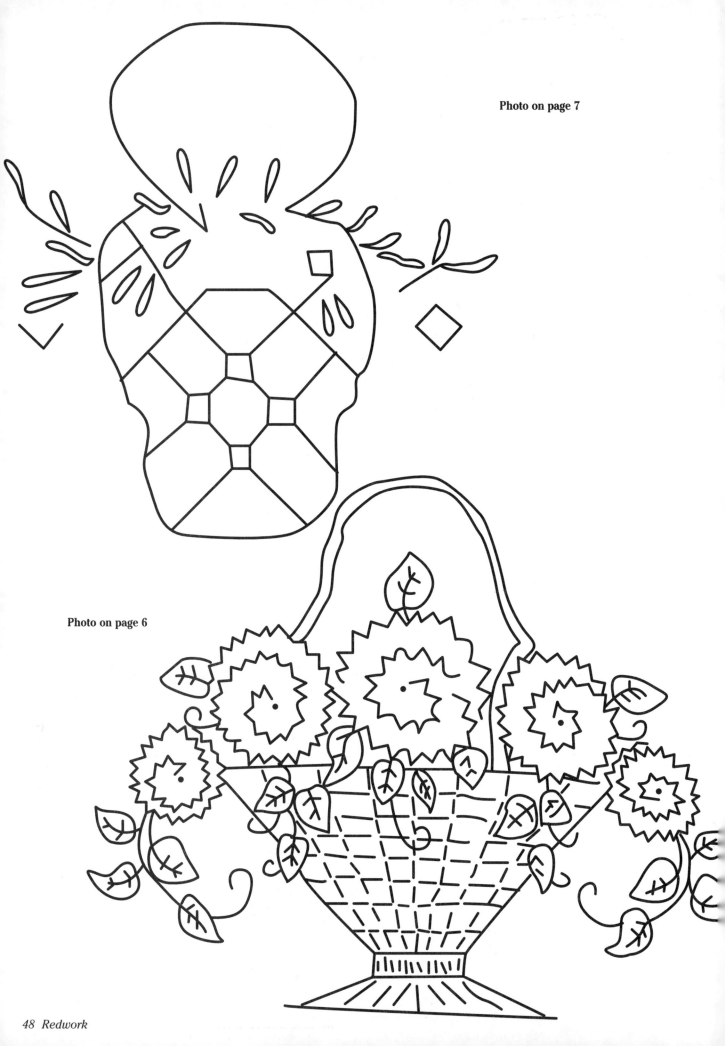

Photo on page 7

Photo on page 6

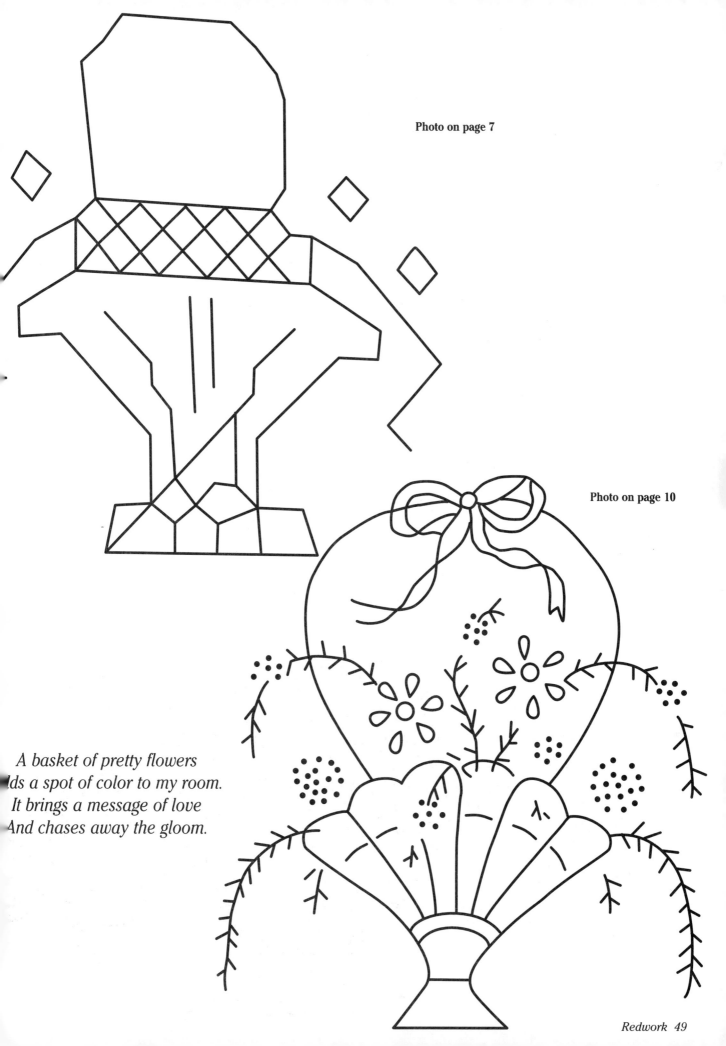

Photo on page 7

Photo on page 10

A basket of pretty flowers
lds a spot of color to my room.
It brings a message of love
And chases away the gloom.

Photo on page 6

Flowers, flowers everywhere
Pick a few for you and some to share.

Photo on page 6

Arlene's favorite
birthday gift on her
10th birthday was
the hope chest
her father had built
in his high school
shop class
20 years before.

A Dutch girl picks tulips
From her garden bright,
Splashes of color in the spring sunlight.

Photo on page 7

Friday

Photo on page 5

Photo on page 7

A Dutch boy wears shoes of wood.
They keep his feet dry
Like nothing else could.

to on page 7

Photo on page 7

Dutch girls wear bonnets shaped funny
To protect their heads
When the day is sunny.

Freddie Frog lives in a bog.
From his seat on a log
He croaks all night
Lost in froggie delight.

Photo on page 10

Photo on page 6

Photo on page 5

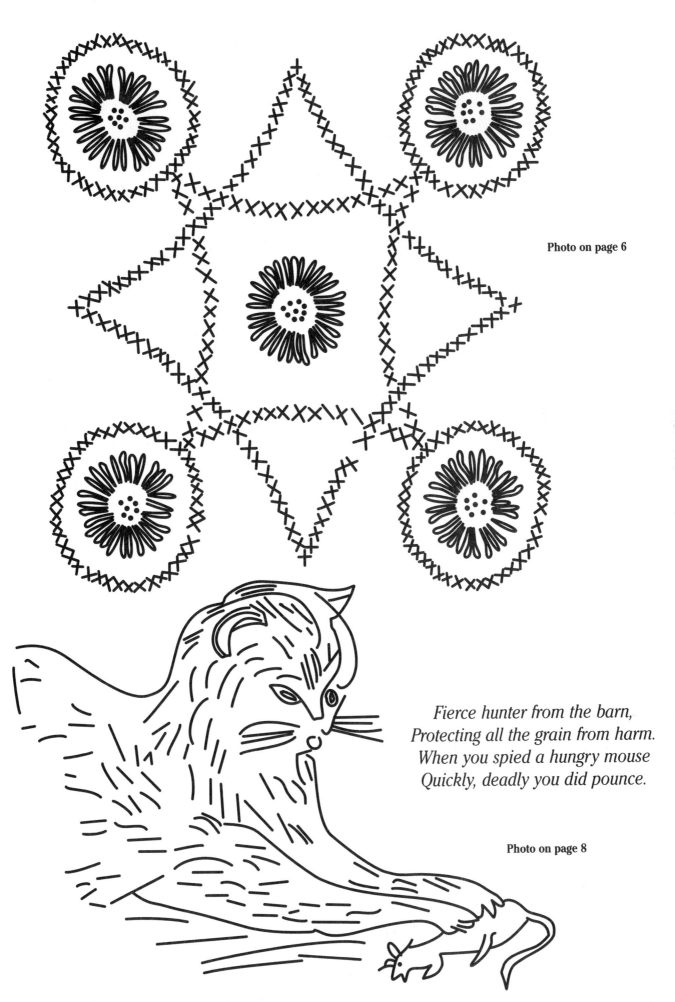

Photo on page 6

Fierce hunter from the barn,
Protecting all the grain from harm.
When you spied a hungry mouse
Quickly, deadly you did pounce.

Photo on page 8

Photo on page 5

During World War II, the Lane Company received many letters from servicemen who wanted to send "cedar chests" to girlfriends or wives back home. The company set up a special Lane correspondence network between servicemen and hometown stores. This service was a wonderful morale booster during wartime.

oct 1913

Little baby sleeping tight
In the darkness of the night
Dream good dreams
And wake to bright sunbeams.

Photo on page 5

Photo on page 10

My love, these flowers I give to thee,
So you may always remember me.

Photo on page 7

Photo on page 5

Summer love blooms in the sun.
Sand and surf are really fun!

SUMMER

Photo on page 10

Photo on page 5

Photo on page 8

Photo on page 5

Photo on page 6

Photo on page 8

Photo on page 7

Photo on page 8

Photo on page 6

*Sunbonnet Sue, Sunbonnet Sue
I'll always, always love you true.*

Photo on page 8

A little girl walks in the sun
Gathering day dreams
And having fun.

Photo on page 6

Lois's husband Bill gave her a "cedar chest" two years before they married. She filled it with the linens her aunts and grandmothers gave to her.

Photo on page 5

Little Betty Blue
In your dress brand new,
Will you play with me
In the shade of the old oak tree?

Little Betty Blue

Photo on page 7

Photo on page 7

Photo on page 5

Photo on page 7

Photo on page 8

Photo on page 8

A boy from Holland is he.
He lives in a land by the sea.
He runs and skates and plays, like

Photo on page 8

Photo on page 7

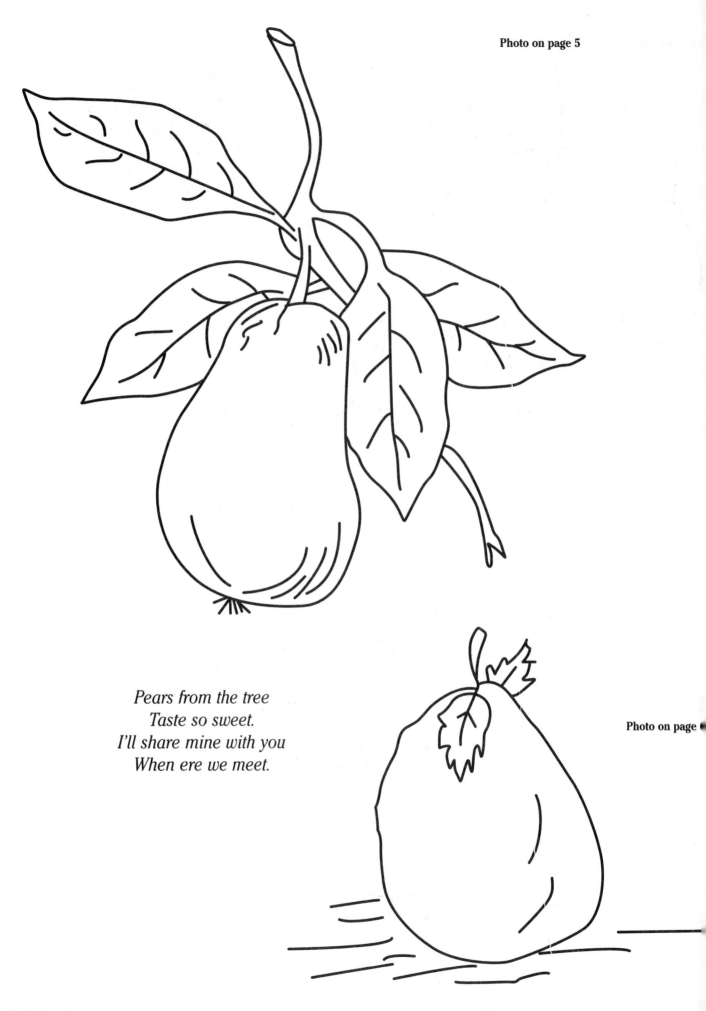

Photo on page 5

Pears from the tree
Taste so sweet.
I'll share mine with you
When ere we meet.

Photo on page ●

Photo on page 7

Since 1930, over 15 million girls have received a free miniature cedar chest from the Lane Company upon graduating from high school.

Photo on page 7

Photo on page 8

Photo on page 8

Photo on page 6

Friends of mine always say,
"An apple a day
Keeps the doctor away."

Photo on page 8

Photo on page 6 and on page 8

If you need someone to talk to
And no one seems to care,
Whistle for your canine companion,
And he'll always be there.

Photo on page 6

Photo on page 10

Photo on page 6

little fox is a creature most sly.
Ie'll tease you and trick you
And then away he will fly.

A sly Fox

Photo on page 8

I AM A

Long before civilizations came,
Proud bison roamed the plains
Providing food, clothing
And protection from the rains.

Photo on page 6

Photo on page 8

Photo on page 6

Photo on page 6

*A camel crosses the desert sands
Bringing treasure from foreign lands.*

Photo on page 6

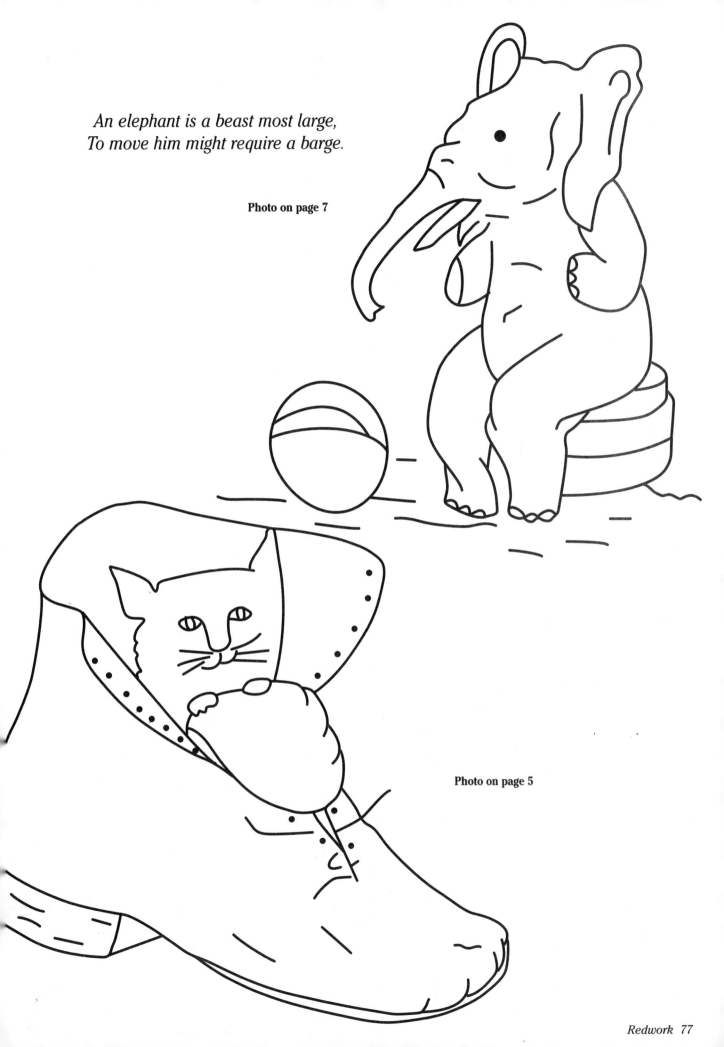

An elephant is a beast most large,
To move him might require a barge.

Photo on page 7

Photo on page 5

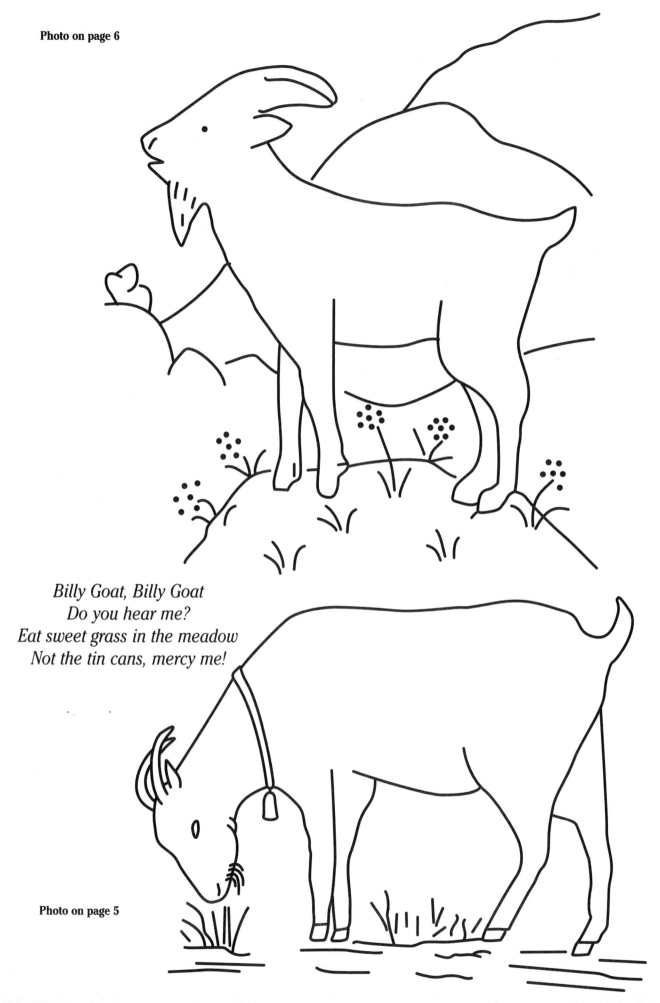

Photo on page 6

Billy Goat, Billy Goat
Do you hear me?
Eat sweet grass in the meadow
Not the tin cans, mercy me!

Photo on page 5

Photo on page 6

The leader of his pride,
A lion stalks the jungle free
Ranging far and wide,
The king of all is he.

Photo on page 6

Photo on page 6

Photo on page 6

*Bears can be both
fierce and scary,
But if it's a teddy, he'll
be soft and merry.*

Photo on page 6

Bears love honey
Yes, it's true.
This may seem funny,
But they really do!

Photo on page 6

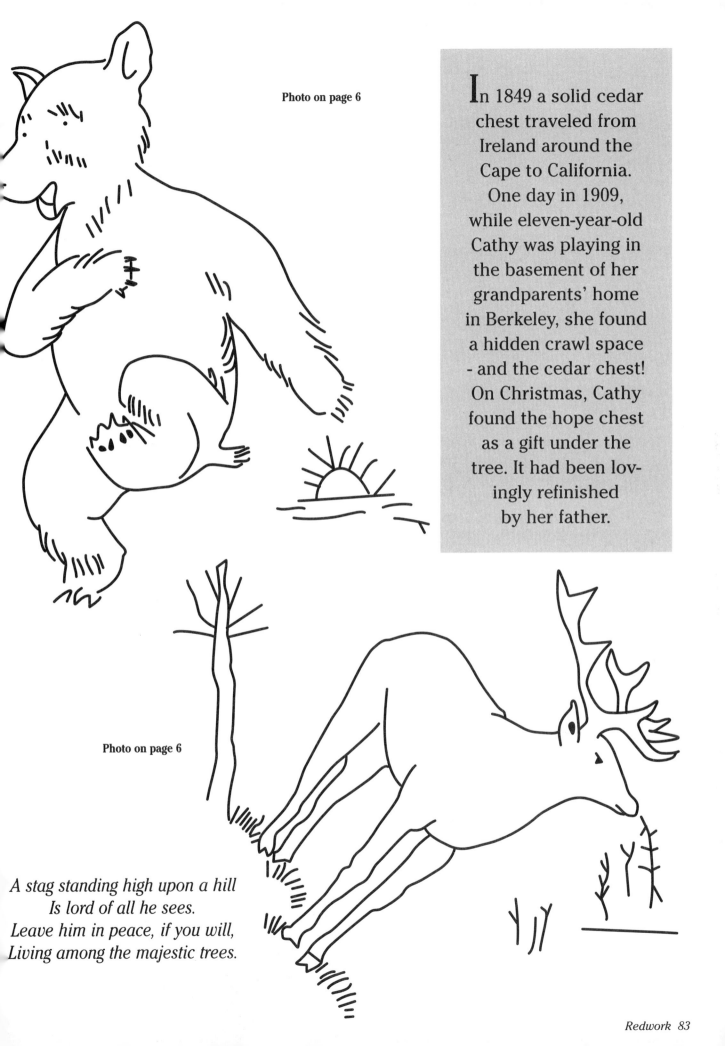

Photo on page 6

In 1849 a solid cedar chest traveled from Ireland around the Cape to California. One day in 1909, while eleven-year-old Cathy was playing in the basement of her grandparents' home in Berkeley, she found a hidden crawl space - and the cedar chest! On Christmas, Cathy found the hope chest as a gift under the tree. It had been lovingly refinished by her father.

Photo on page 6

A stag standing high upon a hill
Is lord of all he sees.
Leave him in peace, if you will,
Living among the majestic trees.

Photo on page 8

Little Red Rabbit
Don't you even dare
To eat all my carrots
And leave my garden bare!

Photo on page 7

Photo on page 6

This squirrel is a very busy beast,
He's not at the autumn feast.
He's working still,
Collecting nuts for winter's chill.

Photo on page 7

Photo on page 5

If I saw a cow jump over the moon,
I'd run inside and hide in my room!

Photo on page 7

Hobby horse, hobby horse
Sitting in my room
You're a better ride, of course
Than my mother's broom.

Photo on page 6

SCISSORS
HOLDER

Leave open →

Leave open →

HEART SACHET - GARLAND - PINCUSHION
INSTRUCTIONS ON PAGE 14

Photo on page 8

*Pretty little kitty
Sitting in the sun.
Wear a perky bow
Just for the fun.*

When Wilna was a young girl, it was common for girls to create and save a dowry of hand-embroidered linens and quilts for when they got married. When she was 8, Wilna embroidered a set of 12 cup towels. In 1929, when Wilna was 12 years old, she saved her allowance for a year. With $25 she purchased her own hope chest (it still has the price sticker inside the lid). Then she filled it with her own hand-stitched linens and quilts.

Polly put the kettle on
The fire is burning bright.
Snow is falling outside
So tea would taste just right.

Pigs squeal,
It's no big deal!
If you feed them fast,
The noise won't last.

APRIL

Photo on page 5

Photo on page 8

Karen inherited a large wooden cedar-lined trunk that was built in Sweden in 1880. The hope chest was filled with linens, quilts and wall hangings. The trunk inspired Karen to stitch heirloom quilts, linens, and doilies to pass down to her children. Two of the original Swedish wall hangings are still in the hope chest her daughter now owns, along with dozens of hand-stitched creations by Karen and her daughter.

Photo on page 8

Sign your name on a
quilt block plain.
Forever be remembered,
It's your own bit of fame.

Photo on page 5

Love me tender,
Love me true.
Come home to me,
Don't leave me blue.

Photo on page 8

Photo on page 8

Photo on page 8

Photo on page 6

Barbara

Photo on page 8

How fast the world moves! Only 50 years ago, young women were preparing linens for household use after they married. There were no paper towels, napkins, disposable wipeables, pre-fabricated sheets nor color-coordinated towels and quilts to decorate their new homes.

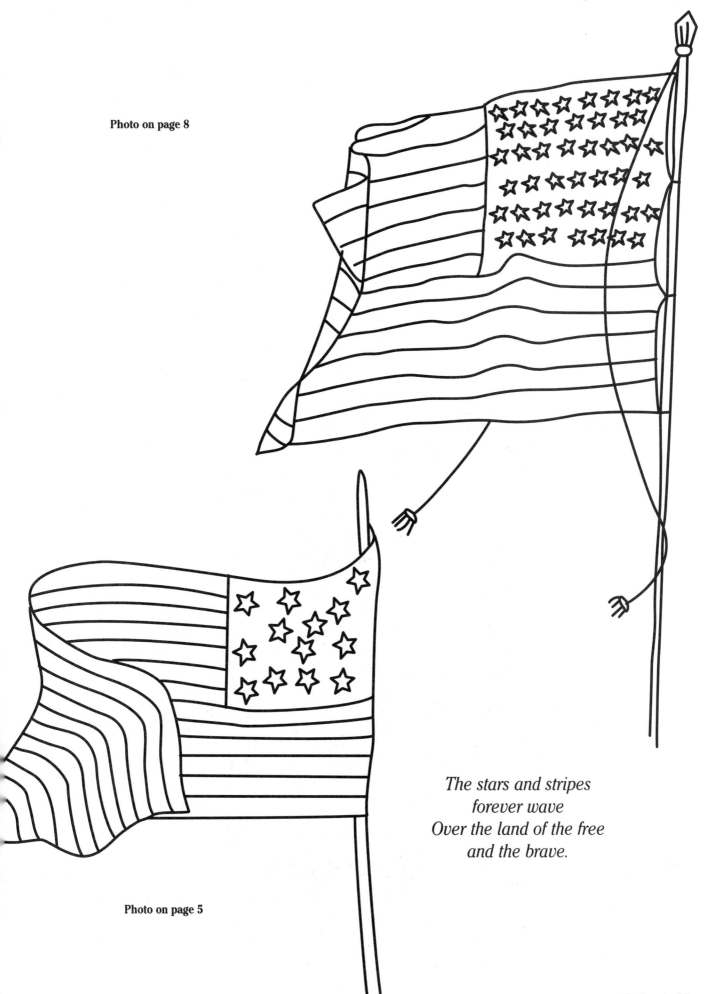

Photo on page 8

*The stars and stripes
forever wave
Over the land of the free
and the brave.*

Photo on page 5

Photo on page 8

The bald eagle proud
with wings unfurled
Is a symbol of strength and freedom
for all the world.